PLANET EARTH FOR KIDS

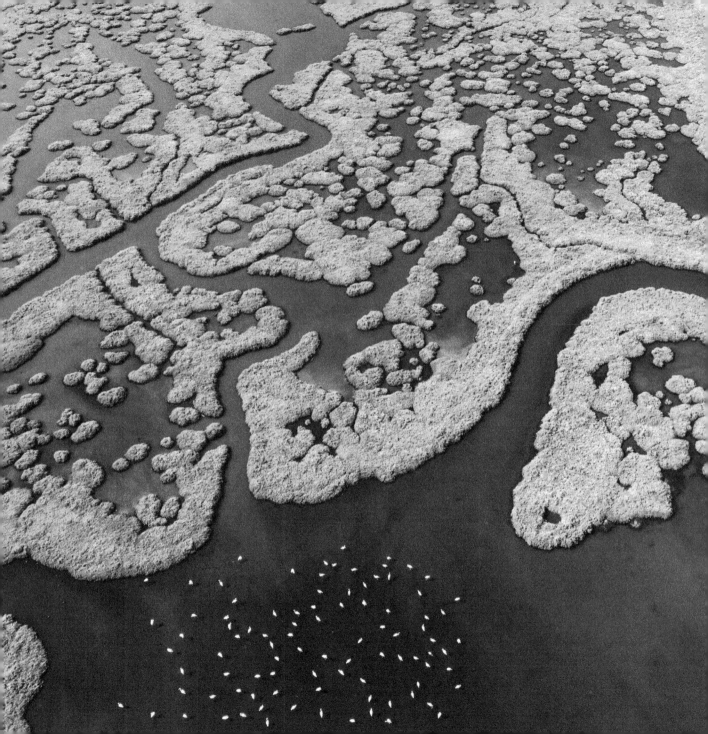

PLANET EARTH
FOR KIDS

A JUNIOR SCIENTIST'S GUIDE
to Water, Air, and Life in
Our Ecosphere

STACY W. KISH, MS

ROCKRIDGE
PRESS

Rockridge Press publishes its books in a variety of electronic and print formats. Some content that appears in print may not be available in electronic books, and vice versa.

TRADEMARKS: Rockridge Press and the Rockridge Press logo are trademarks or registered trademarks of Callisto Media Inc. and/or its affiliates, in the United States and other countries, and may not be used without written permission. All other trademarks are the property of their respective owners. Rockridge Press is not associated with any product or vendor mentioned in this book.

Series Designer: Junior Scientist Design Team
Interior and Cover Designer: Jill Lee
Art Producer: Sue Bischofberger
Editors: Sabrina Young and Nicky Montalvo
Production Manager: Jose Olivera
Production Editor: Melissa Edeburn

Cover photography courtesy of NASA.
Interior photography used under license from iStockPhoto.com, pp. ii, viii–1, 6 (wetland, iceberg, desert, waterfall, mountain, and elephants), 16–17, 24, 25, 26, 27, 36–37, 50–51, and 73; used under license from shutterstock.com, pp. 6 (forest and sea turtle), 25, 26 and 27; © saravutvanset/RooM the Agency/Alamy Stock Photo, p. vi; Norbert Probst/imageBROKER/Alamy Stock Photo, p. 15; Bill Gorum/Alamy Stock Photo, p. 30; Ben Queenborough/Alamy Stock Photo, p. 35; Kip Evans/Alamy Stock Photo, p. 49; courtesy of NASA/SDO, p. 64–65.
Illustrations © 2021 Conor Buckley, pp. 3, 4, 9, 11, 18, 22, 28–31, 38, 41, 42, 44, 45, 52, 54, 57, 58, 60, 67, 70, 71, and 72; used under license from shutterstock.com, pp. 12, 19, 40, 56, and 74; used under license from iStockPhoto.com, p. 21.

ISBN: Print 978-1-64876-642-8 | eBook 978-1-64876-144-7
R0

CONTENTS

Landscape of Guilin, China

WELCOME, JUNIOR SCIENTIST!

Have you ever wondered why some animals live in certain places? Do you want to know what shaped mountains, rivers, and valleys? Are you curious why some places on Earth are warm and others are cool?

This book will answer these questions and show you how our planet became the perfect home for all its plants and animals. We will explore how every part of our surroundings—air, heat, water, and dirt—makes Earth unique. You will dig even deeper into these topics with exciting experiments.

Use a blank notebook or writing pad to record interesting facts you learn along the way. We will study the earth through geology (the study of rocks), meteorology (the study of weather), and ecology (the study of relationships between living things). Get ready for a fun adventure!

Arctic ecosystem

CHAPTER ONE

OUR ECOSYSTEM

All living creatures are organisms. Organisms live all over the world, from the ocean depths to the highest mountain peaks. An ecosystem is a community of interacting organisms—plants and animals—and their physical environment. This chapter explores different kinds of ecosystems and shows us how to study the ways matter (the stuff that makes up everything) and energy flow around the planet. It shows how events, like fire or the disappearance of certain animals, can affect the health of ecosystems. This information can be used to help us protect endangered plants and animals.

What Is an Ecosystem?

The earth is an ecosystem, or a group of organisms and nonliving things that live together in the same area. And Earth, too, is made up of smaller ecosystems that are different sizes and can also be made up of different parts.

Ecosystems can be terrestrial or aquatic and can range from being very small to very big. Terrestrial ecosystems are only found on land and include forests, deserts, grasslands, and tundra (see page 6); they are also part of the coastline (where land and ocean meet). Aquatic ecosystems are made up of a body of water and divided into freshwater and marine ecosystems. Freshwater ecosystems include ponds, rivers, streams, and wetlands. Marine ecosystems include oceans and seas.

An ecosystem is made up of living and nonliving things. Living things include all organisms, like plants, animals, and insects. Each organism plays a role in the ecosystem. Producers, for example, are plants that make their own food during photosynthesis (see page 71). Some organisms, called consumers, eat other plants and animals to live. Tiny organisms, like bacteria and fungi, break down decaying or rotting matter. These organisms are decomposers. They help cycle nutrients around the ecosystem. Nonliving things in an ecosystem include water, soil, rocks, air, and sunlight.

Plant and animal matter are also recycled within the ecosystem. Decomposers break down matter, which then flows through the ecosystem or between different ecosystems. Now the matter can be used again by plants and animals to grow and thrive.

An ecosystem is balanced when the number and types of plants and animals stays the same before and after a change to the environment. Changes could be a fire, the building of a new road, or a flood. A healthy ecosystem does not react too much to environmental changes.

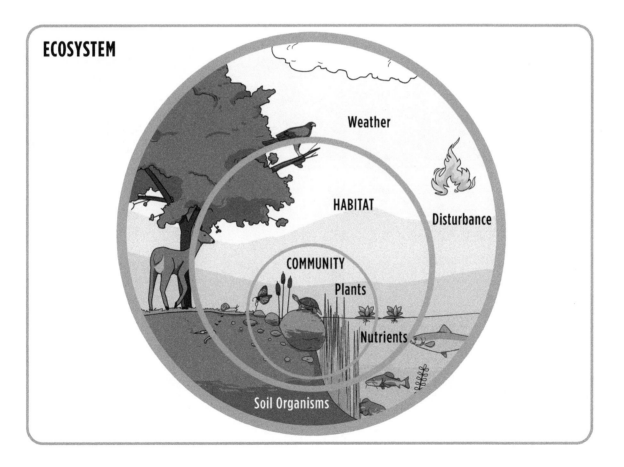

ECOSYSTEM

Weather

HABITAT

Disturbance

COMMUNITY

Plants

Nutrients

Soil Organisms

The Biosphere

The part of an ecosystem where organisms live is called the **biosphere**. "Bio" means life. The biosphere goes from the tallest mountains to miles below the surface of the ocean. It is made up of many ecosystems that interact with one another.

The first organisms on the planet were single-celled organisms, like bacteria. Many of these organisms, like plants, get energy through photosynthesis. Photosynthesis is a way for plants to make their own food. The process also makes oxygen, which plants release into the air. Over time, oxygen collected in the air surrounding Earth, called the **atmosphere**. High in the atmosphere, that oxygen created the *ozone*, a special compound that protects plants and animals from the Sun's harmful rays.

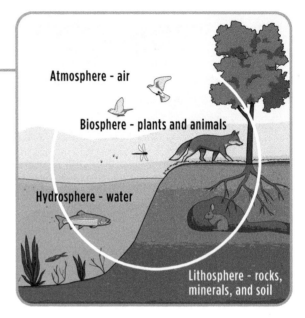

Atmosphere - air

Biosphere - plants and animals

Hydrosphere - water

Lithosphere - rocks, minerals, and soil

All organisms depend on the atmosphere. The atmosphere is mostly made up of gases like nitrogen, oxygen, and argon. Trace gases, like carbon dioxide, can also be found and are important for keeping the planet at a temperature for organisms to live comfortably.

In the biosphere, organisms also interact with the **geosphere** and the **hydrosphere**. The geosphere includes rocks, minerals, and soil on the planet. Organisms live and grow in the soil. They seek shelter in rocks. Minerals also provide nutrients to plants and animals to grow and thrive.

The hydrosphere contains all the water on the planet. Most of the water is saltwater in the oceans and seas. The oceans are home to many organisms. Fresh water, on the other hand, is less than 3 percent of all water on the planet, and most of it is trapped in glaciers and polar ice caps. Organisms can access only a tiny amount of the fresh water available on the planet.

The temperature, oxygen level, elevation (how high something is above sea level), and amount of sunlight all vary inside the biosphere. Most organisms live within the "comfort zone," which is a temperature range that allows life to thrive. This zone goes from 1,640 feet below sea level to 12,300 feet above sea level. Some organisms can live in the deep regions of the ocean with little to no light. Organisms also live in soils and in the mountains high above sea level.

Biomes

The location of an ecosystem or collection of ecosystems on the planet is called a biome. **Biomes** are defined by local **climate** conditions, such as temperature and humidity. They are also made up of the organisms that call them home.

Forest biomes include many types of ecosystems. Tropical forests form along the equator, which is an imaginary line that splits the earth through the middle into its northern and southern hemispheres. Along the equator, it is hot and often very wet. A tropical forest is home to orchids, mosses, and palms. It is also home to birds, bats, small mammals, and insects. Boreal forests, which grow in the mountains at high altitudes, are home to birds, moose, bears, and wolves. Temperate forests, which grow in places where conditions are between those in boreal and tropical forests, are home to many shrubs and trees, as well

as squirrels, rabbits, mountain lions, and black bears.

Grassland biomes are mostly grass rather than trees. The savanna is a grassland biome. It's home to giraffes, kangaroos, snakes, and lions. Temperate grassland biomes are home to gazelles, zebras, rhinoceroses, and prairie dogs. Small trees are also common in temperate grasslands.

Water biomes are defined by how much salt is in their water. There are freshwater biomes and marine biomes. Freshwater biomes are made up of water containing less than 1 percent salt. Those are ponds and lakes, streams and rivers, and wetlands. Fish live in both freshwater and marine biomes. Freshwater fish include trout, bass, and catfish. Freshwater mammals include hippopotamuses, beavers, river otters, and muskrats. Marine biomes contain more than 1 percent of salt in the water. This biome forms the oceans, coral reefs, and estuaries, or places where freshwater mixes with seawater. Marine fish include sharks, swordfish, tuna, and stingrays. Marine mammals include seals, whales, dolphins, and manatees.

Desert biomes are regions that get very little rain each year. There are four kinds of deserts. Hot and dry deserts rarely get rain and grow dry shrubs, like yuccas and ocotillo. Small, burrowing mammals like ground squirrels, burrowing owls, and kangaroo rats live in hot and dry deserts, which are also home to insects, arachnids, reptiles, and birds. Semiarid deserts are hot, get just 0.75 to 1.5 inches of rain every year, and grow cactus and shrubs. Animals like kangaroo rats, rabbits, skunks, and birds live in semiarid deserts. Coastal deserts are not hot and receive 3 to 5 inches of rain every year. Plants there can live in soil with a higher salt content and have learned to retain water during periods of no rain. Coyotes, badgers, amphibians, and reptiles live in coastal deserts. Cold deserts get up to 18 inches of rain every year. Trees that shed their leaves in the fall grow in cold deserts.

These cold deserts are home to jack rabbits, pocket mice, grasshopper mice, and antelopes.

Tundra biomes are cold and get very little rain. They offer few nutrients and have a short growing season. Tundra biomes form at both poles of our planet. Arctic tundra has permanently frozen subsoil, called permafrost, and grows low shrubs and grasses. Arctic tundra is home to caribou, arctic foxes, polar bears, falcons, and mosquitoes. Alpine tundra forms high in the mountains. It is home to plants including grasses and small-leafed shrubs. It is also home to mountain goats, sheep, elk, birds, and insects.

Habitat

A habitat is where an organism lives. The habitat provides organisms with the food, water, shelter, and space they need to survive. It gives plants the proper combination of light, air, water, and soil to grow and thrive. For animals and insects, it also provides a place to find a mate and reproduce.

Not every organism needs the same amount of space. Worker ants have smaller habitat needs than a cougar. A common worker ant lives in a nest with their colony. It does not travel more than 300 feet from the nest in search of food. A cougar is a solitary creature. It may cover 4,800 square feet while hunting for food and searching for a mate.

Plants also have different space needs. Redwood trees that grow along the coast of California can grow more than 350 feet tall. These trees need a lot of space, water, and food compared to lichen. Lichen are small, flat fungi and algae that grow together on rocks. Lichen grows very slowly, less than half an inch per year.

An organism cannot survive without food. Most animals spend a large amount of their time searching for something to eat. Too much food, however, can also be bad. For example, farmers will often add nutrients called fertilizers to the soil to help plants grow. Any fertilizer not used by plants is carried to coastal waters by rivers and streams. Algae in these biomes will then use the fertilizer's nutrients to photosynthesize and grow. The quick growth in algae is called an algal bloom. When the algae die, the bloom sinks into the water and decays. This process uses up the oxygen in the water. Other marine plants and animals cannot survive in oxygen levels that are too low.

All plants and animals need water. Some organisms need more water than others. On land, the available fresh water depends on location and elevation. Many animals follow water throughout the year. For example, gazelles on the savanna travel across the grasslands to find watering holes during the dry season. Plants require a narrow range of water conditions to survive. The water level and salt content in any given spot may shift throughout the year.

Likewise, each organism has different shelter needs. Shelter is another word for a home. In general, a shelter should protect the organism from predators, or animals that kill other animals for food. It should also provide a place where the organism can eat, sleep, hunt, and raise young. Many birds use dead trees for shelter. Burrowing animals, like prairie dogs, create many tunnels underground as shelter.

PRAIRIE DOG HABITAT

CARBON CYCLE

Carbon is an element that is essential for life on Earth. **Inorganic** carbon can be found in many nonliving things, such as the rock limestone, and takes various forms, like gases such as carbon dioxide or carbon monoxide. Inorganic carbon is converted into **organic** carbon during photosynthesis. Organic carbon compounds and molecules are the building blocks of organic matter. Sugar is an example of organic carbon.

The carbon cycle describes the movement of carbon between organic and inorganic forms. As carbon cycles through ecosystems, it is made available for organisms. Inorganic carbon may also be locked away in rocks and fossil fuels, such as coal, natural gas, and oil. When fossil fuels are burned, they release ancient carbon dioxide into the atmosphere. Carbon dioxide traps solar radiation near Earth's surface. As the amount of carbon dioxide increases in the atmosphere, the planet gets warmer.

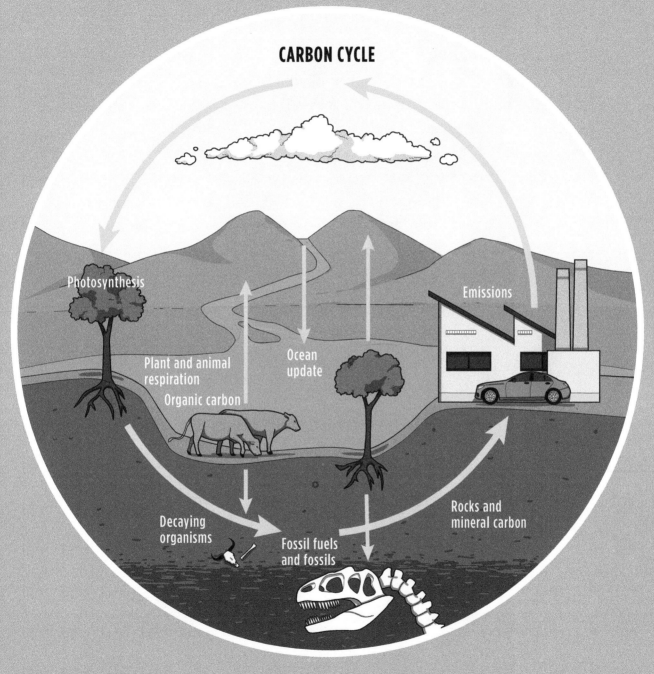

CARBON CYCLE

Photosynthesis

Plant and animal
respiration

Organic carbon

Ocean
update

Emissions

Decaying
organisms

Fossil fuels
and fossils

Rocks and
mineral carbon

ARE YOU AN ECOSYSTEM?

Yes! You are an ecosystem. Your body is home to trillions of bacteria. Bacteria comprise around 0.3 percent of your body mass. These bacteria make up the human microbiome. Your skin makes up one of the largest regions on your body that interacts with bacteria. This means your skin is like the outer shell of the earth and bacteria are like plants living on the surface. Deeper within your body, bacteria also live in your intestines, where they help you remove nutrients from the food you eat and remain healthy. Bacteria also interact with your immune system. They help it recognize dangerous invaders and fight off other disease-causing bacteria and viruses. Although bacteria often get a bad rap, most are quite beneficial and keep you healthy.

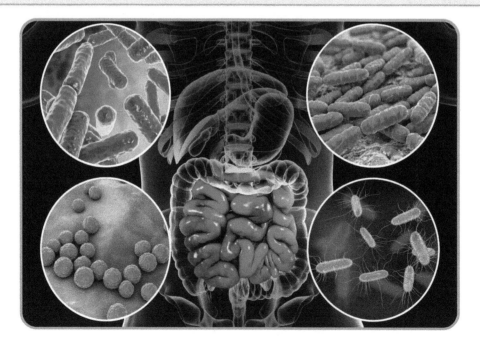

CREATE A CLOSED ECOSYSTEM

You can create an ecosystem that fits in the palm of your hand with just seven items.

What You'll Need:

CLEAN, AIRTIGHT GLASS MASON JAR WITH LID

CLEAN AQUARIUM SAND

ACTIVATED CHARCOAL

SOIL

PLANTS

SMALL ROCKS OR MOSS

WATER

What to Do:

1. Put about 1 to 2 inches of clean sand in the bottom of the jar.

2. Add about ½ inch of activated charcoal.

3. Add 2 to 4 inches of soil.

4. Add plants to the biosphere and decorate it with small rocks or moss.

5. Seal the jar with the lid.

6. Place the biosphere near a window but not in direct sunlight.

7. Observe the biosphere over the next few days and weeks. Take note of water vapor, plant growth, and other interesting changes that might occur.

ECOSYSTEM SPOTLIGHT

A food web is a way to visualize how organisms interact in an eco-system. Producers (see page 2) form the base of the food web. Phytoplankton are the plants, or producers, in the ocean. As one moves higher up the food web, producers are eaten by first-, second-, and third-level consumers. In the ocean, these consumers can include small fish, crustaceans, larger fish, and small sharks. Most ecosystems contain top-level predators that are not hunted or eaten by any other organisms. Decomposers eat the leftover scraps remaining in each level of the ecosystem.

Porcelain Crab fishing for plankton

Rock formations in Bisti Badlands, New Mexico

CHAPTER TWO

EARTH

The surface of the planet is constantly changing. Forces that are deep within the planet are partly responsible for shaping the earth's surface. These forces can create and destroy mountains, volcanoes, and even trenches in the oceans. The earth's surface can also be shaped by weather, plants, and animals, which break rock into smaller pieces that are transported to other areas by water, wind, ice, and even gravity. These forces smooth and level the planet's landscape, reshaping it time and time again.

Structure

Earth formed 4.5 billion years ago. At the time, the planet was partially liquid, or molten. Within this liquid **magma**, heavy elements sank toward the center of the planet, and light elements floated toward the top. Eventually, the earth cooled enough so that this magma became solid, although some parts of the planet's core are still liquid today.

This process of heating and cooling created a planet with distinct layers.

CORE

The core lies 2,000 miles below the earth's surface. It is made up mostly of nickel and iron. It is unusual because the inner core is solid while the outer core is liquid.

The outer core is a thick, gooey liquid metal, the flowing of which

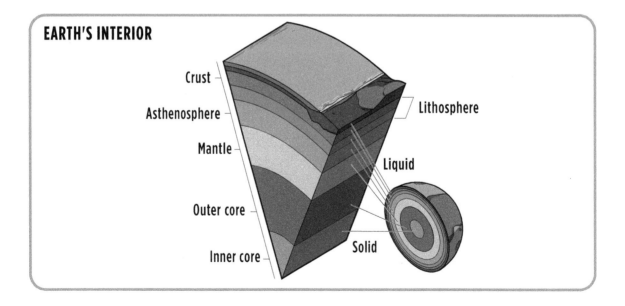

EARTH'S INTERIOR

Crust
Asthenosphere
Mantle
Outer core
Inner core
Lithosphere
Liquid
Solid

produces Earth's magnetic field. The earth's magnetic field extends outward into space and protects the planet from a stream of charged particles coming from the Sun. Without this protection, the charged particles would damage the ozone layer and harm life on Earth.

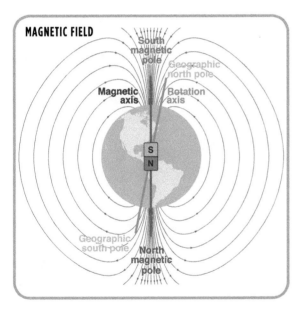

MANTLE

The mantle is the largest part of Earth's interior. It is 1,800 miles thick and varies in temperature. It is close to 1,200 degrees Fahrenheit near the crust and warms to 6,700 degrees Fahrenheit near the core.

As the planet formed, the heavy elements sank to the core. The rest of the material stayed in the mantle. Over time, water in the mantle has been released to the planet's surface during volcanic eruptions. This process has continually changed the chemistry of the mantle. Today, the mantle is made up of minerals that are rich in silica and oxygen. Minerals are the building blocks for rocks. Mantle rocks are solid, but the high temperature causes the rocks to move like silly putty.

The upper mantle is a very important piece of the mantle. It starts at the base of the crust and continues to around 250 miles below Earth's surface. The lithosphere is a combination of rigid crust and upper mantle. The lithosphere is split into plates that move over the asthenosphere, which is a more liquid part of the upper mantle. Plate tectonics is the movement of these plates across the planet's surface (see page 21). This process reshapes the planet's surface. It can create new continents, oceans, and mountains, and it can also produce earthquakes and volcanoes.

CRUST

The crust is the solid outer layer of the planet. It is the most visible portion of the planet and where most organisms live. The crust is made up of minerals that are rich in silica and oxygen. There are two types of crust—continental crust and oceanic crust. Oceanic crust is thin, about 5 miles thick. It is mostly made up of minerals rich in the elements iron and manganese. Continental crust is thicker, about 25 miles thick. It is made up of minerals rich in the elements silicon and potassium.

WHY IS THE EARTH ROUND?

Our planet has a **gravitational force** that pulls everything inward. It's what keeps our feet on the ground and it also gives Earth its shape. Earth is an oblate spheroid, which is a fancy way of saying that the poles are flattened and the equator bulges. This odd shape is caused by the planet's rotation. As the planet spins, its mass is pushed outward due to centrifugal force. If you've ever been on a carnival ride or a roller coaster, you have felt the push of centrifugal force. The force is strongest along the equator, which is farthest away from the axis where the earth spins. That's why the planet bulges outward along the equator more than at the poles. The strength of gravity is slightly weaker at the equator than the poles.

Plate Tectonics

Our planet has five oceans that separate seven continents. The planet's surface is constantly changing. Plate tectonics explain this slow but constant change. A plate can either be only oceanic lithosphere or a combination of continental and oceanic lithosphere. Plates move at different speeds across the planet's surface.

Plate tectonics shape Earth's surface along plate boundaries. There are three types of plate boundaries—convergent, divergent, and transform.

Convergent plate boundaries describe two plates moving together. When two plates made up of continental crust come together, both plates move upward. This creates mountains. An oceanic plate is denser than a continental plate, so when they meet, the oceanic plate moves below the continental plate. This will produce an

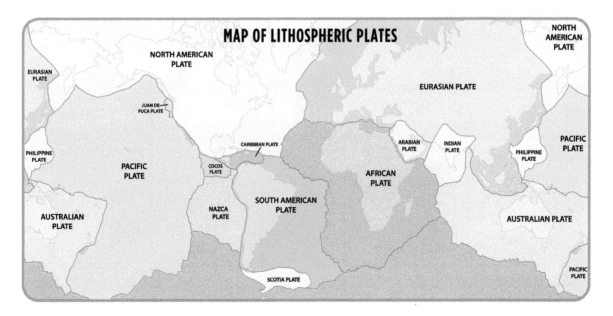

MAP OF LITHOSPHERIC PLATES

NORTH AMERICAN PLATE

EURASIAN PLATE

JUAN DE FUCA PLATE

PHILIPPINE PLATE

PACIFIC PLATE

AUSTRALIAN PLATE

NAZCA PLATE

COCOS PLATE

CARIBBEAN PLATE

SOUTH AMERICAN PLATE

AFRICAN PLATE

ARABIAN PLATE

INDIAN PLATE

PHILIPPINE PLATE

EURASIAN PLATE

NORTH AMERICAN PLATE

PACIFIC PLATE

AUSTRALIAN PLATE

PACIFIC PLATE

SCOTIA PLATE

oceanic trench, or a deep ditch in the ocean. When an oceanic plate meets another oceanic plate, the older, denser plate moves below and makes an even deeper trench.

Divergent plate boundaries are where two plates move apart. When a continental plate breaks apart, a rift valley forms. East Africa is a region that is currently rifting apart. The rifting process has exposed ancient rock at Earth's surface, revealing long-buried archaeological and paleontological discoveries. As the rifting continental crust gets thinner, magma will erupt as lava at Earth's surface. Over time, a new ocean basin will form.

Transform plate boundaries form where two **tectonic plates** move horizontally past each other. No crust is created or destroyed at a transform boundary. These boundaries are characterized by long faults, such as the San Andreas Fault, that cause large earthquakes.

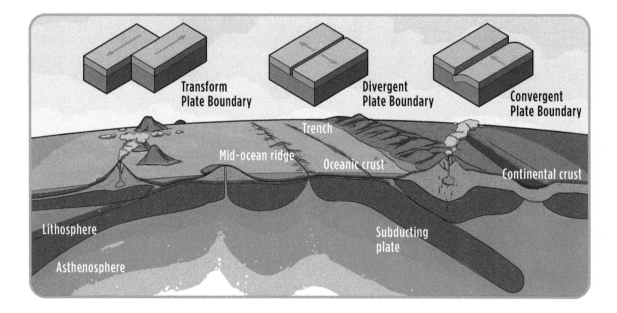

VOLCANOES

Volcanoes are mountains that form along the boundaries where tectonic plates come together and pull apart. **Lava**, or molten rock, melts through the rock and spills out at Earth's surface. When tectonic plates collide, oceanic crust is recycled back into the upper mantle. Water transported within this crust enters the mantle and causes it to melt. This molten material melts through the overlying continental crust. It forms a line of volcanoes that follows the shape of the coastline. Volcanoes that no longer erupt are extinct. Volcanoes that continue to erupt are active. Volcanoes that erupt infrequently are dormant. Volcanoes that form where tectonic plates come together produce explosive and dangerous eruptions.

Volcanoes that form where tectonic plates pull apart can be found on land and in the ocean. They can form long chains of underwater volcanoes. When these volcanoes erupt, hot magma rises to the surface, creating lava. The lava at the surface cools to form new oceanic crust. These eruptions are nearly continuous and quiet.

EARTHQUAKES

Rocks in the earth's crust can contain large fractures, or breaks, called faults. Earthquakes occur when stress builds up over long periods of time but is released quickly, allowing rocks to move against each other along faults. The energy released during an earthquake moves across and through the planet. Earthquakes can happen close to Earth's surface or deep within the crust. They can cause a lot of damage, depending on how strong they are.

LANDSLIDES

Earthquakes can sometimes trigger landslides. A landslide is the mass movement of rocks and soil down a slope. On April 25, 2015, a 7.8 magnitude earthquake rocked the mountainous country of Nepal, triggering devastating landslides. These events blocked rivers, trapped communities, and impaired the ability of rescue personnel to get supplies to those affected.

Rocks and Minerals

The earth's crust is composed of rocks and **minerals**. A mineral is a solid crystal. A crystal is made up of a specific set of elements in an orderly arrangement. Rocks can be made up of one type or many different types of minerals. There are three types of rocks: igneous, metamorphic, and sedimentary.

IGNEOUS

Igneous rock forms from molten magma inside the earth or lava at Earth's surface. Igneous rocks are defined by what they are made of and where they form. Mafic igneous rocks are rich in iron and magnesium. Felsic igneous rocks are rich in potassium and silicon.

Igneous rocks can form inside Earth or on its surface. Intrusive igneous rocks form inside the earth. Magma cools slowly, causing large mineral crystals to grow. Examples of intrusive rocks are gabbro and granite. Extrusive igneous rocks form at Earth's surface. The lava cools quickly, causing small mineral crystals to form. Examples of extrusive igneous rocks are rhyolite and basalt. When lava cools extremely quickly, a glass, like obsidian, forms. Pumice is also an extrusive igneous rock that cools quickly. The small holes in the rock form when air escapes as the rock cools.

Basalt

Gabbro

Diorite

Rhyolite

Pumice

Pegmatite

Obsidian

Granite

METAMORPHIC

Metamorphic rocks form when a preexisting rock is changed by temperature and/or pressure. They are either foliated or non-foliated rocks.

A foliated metamorphic rock has minerals that grow perpendicular (at a 90-degree angle) to a source of pressure. As the pressure increases, the minerals grow longer and thicker. During **metamorphism**, sedimentary rocks (such as shale) form a series of foliated rocks. As the intensity of pressure and temperature increase, shale is transformed into metamorphic rocks, such as slate, phyllite, schist, and gneiss.

Non-foliated metamorphic rocks form when mineral growth is not determined by pressure. Limestone, a sedimentary rock, when exposed to pressure and/or temperature is metamorphosed to marble. Sandstone is metamorphosed to quartzite.

Phyllite **Quartzite** **Slate**

Gneiss **Marble** **Schist** **Hornfels**

SEDIMENTARY

Sedimentary rocks form from eroded fragments of preexisting rocks. They may also form when minerals precipitate, or grow out of water. Sedimentary rocks are classified as clastic, organic, or chemical.

Clastic sedimentary rocks form when other rocks are weathered. The rock fragments are transported to another location by wind, water, ice, or even gravity. Over time, the fragments are compressed and cemented together to form a sedimentary rock, such as shale or sandstone.

Unlike clastic sedimentary rocks that form from fragments of other rocks and minerals, organic sedimentary rocks form from fragments of dead organisms. In both, the fragments are cemented together to produce sedimentary rock. Organic sedimentary rocks include chalk and coal.

Chemical sedimentary rocks are created when minerals form from water.

Limestone	Shale	Flint	Sandstone
Coal	Chert	Conglomerate	Rock Salt

The small minerals build up to create a rock. Chemical sedimentary rocks include rock salt and chert.

Rock Cycle

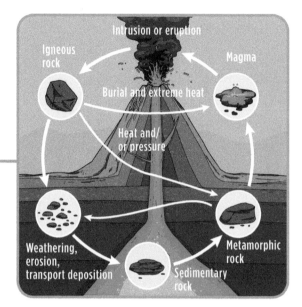

The rock cycle describes the transition of one type of rock to another. Follow the graphic to explore all of the processes that cause transitions between the different rock types.

WEATHERING AND EROSION

Weathering is the process of breaking a rock into smaller particles. These pieces are called sediment. Sediments vary in size. The sediment with the smallest grain size is clay. Each grain of clay is smaller than the thickness of a human hair. The largest sediment is a boulder, which is bigger than a basketball. Physical weathering is the mechanical breakdown of rocks into sediments by ice, wind, plant roots, and animals. Chemical weathering weakens minerals in a rock using water, acid, or oxygen. As the minerals weaken, the rock can crumble or dissolve.

Erosion is the movement of sediment away from the place where it forms. Erosion typically carries sediment from a higher elevation to a lower elevation. This process also exposes fresh rock surface for additional weathering. Together, weathering and erosion reduce the elevation of the overall landscape. One example of an erosional feature is a river valley.

Erosion may transport sediment by gravity, water, wind, or glaciers. The size and distance a grain of sediment is eroded depends on the energy of the wind, water, or glacier. For example, fast-moving water can transport pebbles, cobbles, and even boulders. Wind typically transports fine sand, silt, and clay.

Eroded sediment can be carried by suspension, saltation, or traction. Suspension occurs when wind or water carries a sediment grain without the grain touching the ground. Saltation describes a hopping process. The wind or water will lift and carry the sediment a short distance. The sediment settles back on the ground. The wind or water then picks the grain up again. This process happens over and over again. Traction describes how wind or water pushes a sediment grain along the ground.

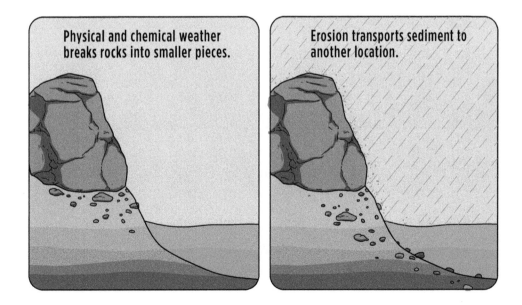

Physical and chemical weather breaks rocks into smaller pieces.

Erosion transports sediment to another location.

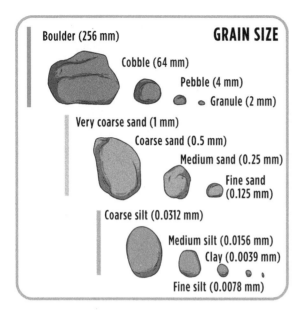

GRAIN SIZE

Boulder (256 mm)

Cobble (64 mm)

Pebble (4 mm)

Granule (2 mm)

Very coarse sand (1 mm)

Coarse sand (0.5 mm)

Medium sand (0.25 mm)

Fine sand (0.125 mm)

Coarse silt (0.0312 mm)

Medium silt (0.0156 mm)

Clay (0.0039 mm)

Fine silt (0.0078 mm)

Deposition occurs at the end of the erosion process, when the sediment settles in a resting place. Deposition can happen at the place where a river enters another body of water. As the water slows, it loses energy and sediments are deposited. Coarse or large sediment grains are generally deposited first. Fine or small sediment grains are generally deposited later. As the sediment is deposited, it forms depositional features, such as an alluvial fan. An alluvial fan typically forms at the base of a steep valley. A seasonal stream carries sediment down the steep slope. The fan forms as coarse and then fine sediment settles on the ground.

PHOSPHORUS CYCLE

The **phosphorus** cycle is similar to the carbon cycle (page 10). As the element phosphorus moves around the planet, it changes from an inorganic form to an organic form and back again. Phosphorus is important for cell development and plays a role in how molecules store and use energy.

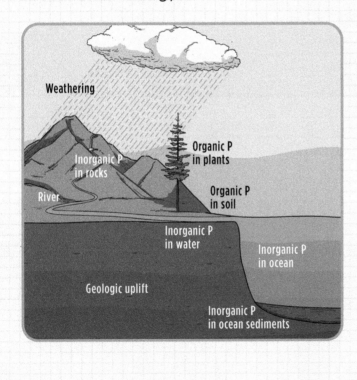

Phosphorus is released from rocks by weathering and carried to soil by erosion. Plants absorb the inorganic phosphorus and change it to an organic form necessary for them to grow. Animals eat plants to get organic phosphorus. When a plant or animal dies, its phosphorus is released back into the soil. Bacteria in the soil change the organic phosphorus back into an inorganic form.

BUILD A MOUNTAIN

Topography describes the elevation of a landform above sea level. A topographic map is drawn with contour lines as a way to illustrate three-dimensional objects on a two-dimensional page. Contour lines represent a line of equal elevation. The contour interval provides the unit of change from one contour line to the next.

In this activity, you will create a topographic map of a mountain.

What You'll Need:

CLAY

A RULER

DENTAL FLOSS

PAPER

A PENCIL

What to Do:

1. Create a 5-inch-high mountain with clay. Use the ruler to measure the height.

2. Cut a strand of dental floss long enough to fit across the mountain and to wrap around your index fingers.

3. Slice the clay mountain horizontally into ½-inch-thick pieces with the dental floss.

4. Place the largest slice on the paper and trace around its perimeter, or all around its edge, then remove the slice from the paper.

5. Place the next largest slice in the center of the previous shape, trace its perimeter, and remove it from the paper. Repeat this with all of the remaining slices.

6. Count the number of slices in the clay model.

7. Divide the height of the mountain (5 inches) by the number of slices in the model (from step 6). This value is called the *contour interval*; it represents the change in elevation on a flat map.

8. Write the contour interval value on the map.

ECOSYSTEM SPOTLIGHT

The tundra extends across the Arctic. It remains cold and dry throughout the year, receiving less than 10 inches of precipitation, like snow or sometimes rain. It has a short growing season—only 10 weeks. Most of the soil is frozen. There are no trees, but the tundra is populated by small shrubs, grasses, mosses, and lichens. Animals living on the tundra have adapted to the harsh conditions. Common wildlife includes small mammals, like lemmings, hares, and ground squirrels. It is also home to larger animals, like caribou, arctic foxes, snowy owls, and polar bears. Insects have also adapted to the cold. Their blood contains a chemical compound like antifreeze that keeps their bodily fluids liquid when the temperature dips below freezing.

The rising temperature of the earth's surface is negatively affecting the tundra. Frozen soil is thawing and the trapped organic matter is beginning to decay, releasing ancient carbon dioxide and methane into the atmosphere. This process drives further heating of the atmosphere and continued thawing of the permafrost in the future.

Polar bear in the Arctic tundra

Close-up of an ocean wave

CHAPTER THREE

WATER

Earth is often called the blue planet because 70 percent of the planet's surface is covered by water. Only a small amount of this water is fresh and available to drink. Most fresh water is locked away in ice. It also flows underground. The rest flows across Earth's surface, ultimately returning to the ocean. This cycle transfers the small amount of fresh water through the ecosystem, sharing it with plants and animals in the biosphere. The movement of water is also responsible for weather and precipitation, such as rain. Rain erodes the landscapes. By exploring these interactions, we can understand where water is located and why it is such a precious resource on the planet.

The Hydrosphere

The solar system lacks water. Like other planets in the solar system, the young Earth also lacked water. The planet formed 4.5 billion years ago. By studying rocks, we can see that oceans formed on the planet at least four billion years ago. The best explanation for how water came to be is that a combination of gases, released during volcanic eruptions and collisions with comets from outer space, delivered water to our

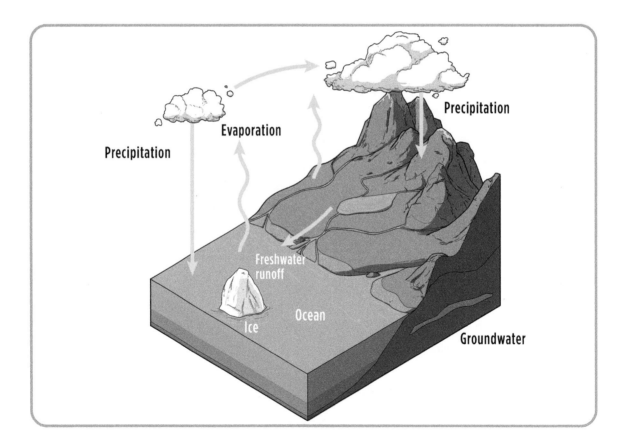

planet's surface. Today, the hydrosphere, which includes all water on the planet, is an important part of Earth's ecosystem.

Water in the hydrosphere passes through the atmosphere as water vapor. This gaseous form of water is as invisible as the air we breathe, yet water vapor is the backbone of weather. When water vapor cools, it turns into liquid water to form precipitation, like rain. If this rain freezes as it falls to the ground, it becomes snow or hail. The precipitation washes over the land and wears down rocks by physical and chemical weathering, breaking rocks into smaller fragments. Rivers and streams redistribute sediment. Ice also digs into the landscape, eroding the surface of the planet.

Oceans

The global ocean is divided into five separate bodies of water, most of which have large landmasses between them. They are the Atlantic Ocean, the Indian Ocean, the Pacific Ocean, the Arctic Ocean, and the Southern Ocean. The five oceans are interconnected, and water flows freely from one to another.

The salt in ocean water is actually dissolved ions, which are charged atoms or molecules derived from minerals on land. The most common ions in saltwater are chloride and sodium. As rocks and minerals are weathered, the ions are carried by rivers and streams to the ocean. The ions increase the salinity, or saltiness, of ocean water. On average, ocean water has a salinity of about 35. That means there are 35 parts of salt (ions) for 1,000 parts of water.

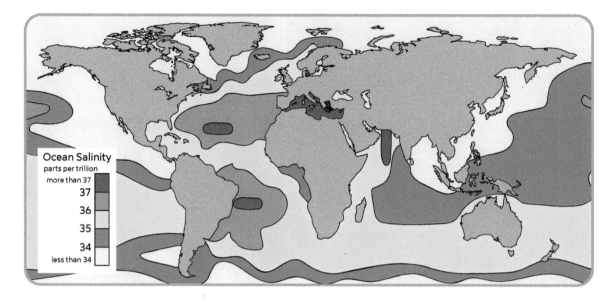

Ocean Salinity
parts per trillion
more than 37
37
36
35
34
less than 34

Although salt makes up only a tiny fraction of ocean water, it makes ocean water unhealthy to drink. The salt content in ocean water is too high for the human body to process. If someone drank ocean water, they'd have to urinate more water than they drank in order to get rid of the extra salt in their body. They would only get thirstier and dehydrate.

Streams and Lakes

Fresh water only makes up around 3 percent of the water on the surface of the planet. Most of the fresh water is trapped in glacial ice in polar and mountainous regions and flows through rocks as groundwater. Humans tap into the rest of the fresh water that flows across Earth's surface. This water is mostly found in streams, rivers, ponds, and lakes.

A stream is a body of water in motion. It flows downhill from its source and follows the shape of the landscape to a larger body of water, like a lake or ocean. Streams may be called different things depending on their size, depth, speed, and location. Other common names include creeks, brooks, tributaries, bayous, and rivers. Streams have had historical importance for human evolution by providing a method for travel, trade, food, defense, waste disposal, and recreation.

A pond is a small body of fresh water that is fed by underwater springs. A lake is a larger and deeper body of fresh water. Water usually drains from a lake into a river. Whereas lakes and ponds are completely surrounded by land, bays are bodies of water that are only partly enclosed by land. They lead directly into the ocean.

Groundwater is the fresh water that moves through small spaces in rocks, such as cracks and pores. These reservoirs are called aquifers. People tap into

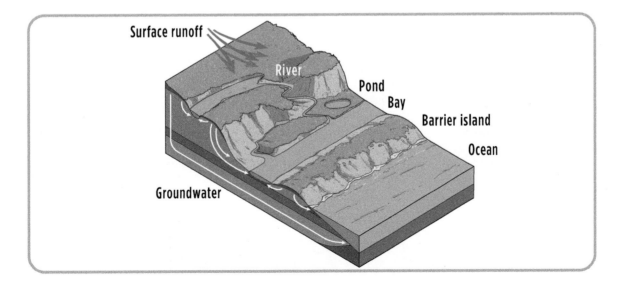

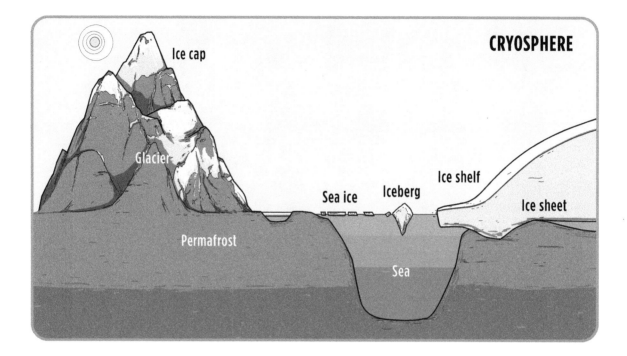

CRYOSPHERE

Ice cap

Glacier

Permafrost

Sea ice

Iceberg

Ice shelf

Ice sheet

Sea

aquifers as a source of drinking water. As precipitation falls on Earth's surface, some water seeps back through the soil, replenishing groundwater slowly over time.

The **cryosphere** includes all the frozen fresh water in the hydrosphere—ice caps, glaciers, permafrost, sea ice, and snow. The cryosphere plays a critical role in the climate system. Ice and snow reflect incoming sunlight back into space. As the planet warms, the cryosphere melts and shrinks. Less sunlight is reflected into space and the planet continues to warm.

Clouds and Rain

Water vapor is invisible in the atmosphere. It is essential in the creation of clouds and precipitation. To start, air moves across the planet's surface in separate bubbles, called parcels. As a warm parcel of air rises into the atmosphere, the atmospheric pressure decreases and the gases within the parcel expand. As air rises, it also cools. As the air cools, water vapor in the air turns into liquid water, forming the base of a cloud. At this point, the air parcel rises more slowly.

Clouds are classified by their altitude and shape. Stratus clouds are thick, flat, and featureless. These clouds occur only in the lower levels of the atmosphere. This type of cloud typically forms light, gentle precipitation. Cumulus clouds also form in the lower atmosphere but grow higher than stratus clouds. They look like cotton balls and are often described as puffy in appearance. Cumulus clouds can be solitary or appear in lines or clusters. Cumulus clouds can bring heavy rain, lightning, and thunder. Cirrus clouds form high in the atmosphere. They are composed of ice crystals and appear wispy.

Clouds can be described even more with a few prefixes. The prefix (before a word) "nimbo" or suffix (after a word) "nimbus" is added to a cloud that produces rain. A cumulonimbus cloud brings heavy rain. The prefix "alto" describes clouds that form at 6,000 feet above Earth's surface. An altostratus cloud is a thick, blanket-like cloud high in the atmosphere. The prefix "cirro" describes clouds that form higher than 19,000 feet above Earth's surface. A cirrostratus cloud is a thin, blanket-like cloud high in the atmosphere.

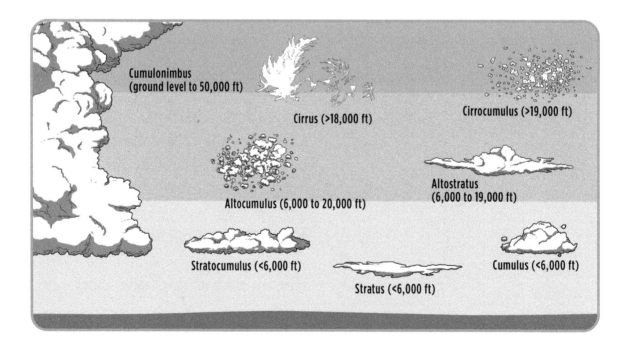

Cumulonimbus (ground level to 50,000 ft)

Cirrus (>18,000 ft)

Cirrocumulus (>19,000 ft)

Altocumulus (6,000 to 20,000 ft)

Altostratus (6,000 to 19,000 ft)

Stratocumulus (<6,000 ft)

Stratus (<6,000 ft)

Cumulus (<6,000 ft)

WATER CYCLE

Water moves through three phases—gas, liquid, and solid—in a repeating cycle, at or close to the planet's surface. For example, when liquid water evaporates from a body of water, it warms and turns into a gas (water vapor), which rises in the atmosphere. When water vapor cools at a higher and colder part of the atmosphere, it condenses to form liquid fresh water in the atmosphere that turns into rain. If the water is high up in the atmosphere, it'll be so cold that the water turns to solid ice by freezing. As the ice falls into a lower and warmer atmosphere, it melts to form liquid water. The water cycle replenishes fresh water throughout the ecosystem.

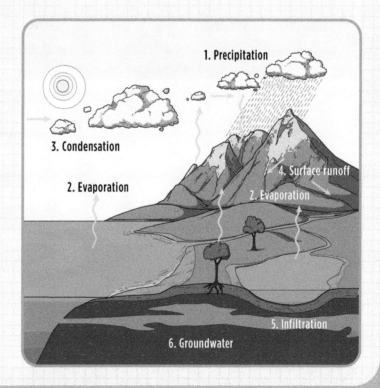

1. Precipitation
3. Condensation
2. Evaporation
4. Surface runoff
2. Evaporation
5. Infiltration
6. Groundwater

START A FLOOD

How could a flood affect your home? In this activity, you will create a landscape, then explore what happens when a flood occurs. Use the materials below to construct a cardboard house.

What You'll Need:

WATERPROOF CONTAINER OR SHALLOW PLASTIC STORAGE CONTAINER (1 FOOT BY 3 FEET)

ROCKS

SAND

CARDBOARD, 1-FOOT-SQUARE SHEET

PLANTS

WATER BOTTLE

NEWSPAPER

WATER

What to Do:

1. Place some rocks and sand into the container, as much as you need to create a landscape. Arrange the rocks and sand to form hills and valleys. Leave a space open along one edge of the container. The gap will serve as the location of a river.

2. Build several small houses using the cardboard. Place plants around the neighborhood.

3. Slowly add water to the river and observe.

4. Continue to add more water to the river until it overflows the bank.

5. Stop adding water and observe what happens. In particular, look at what happens as the water overflows the riverbank. How does the water affect the homes and plants? What does the water do to the surrounding landscape?

ECOSYSTEM SPOTLIGHT

A tide pool is a unique ecosystem. It marks the transition between marine and land environments in the intertidal zone along a coastline. The highest portion of the tide pool is only underwater during high tide. Mussels, sea lettuce, and sea stars often live in the highest portion. The middle portion of the tide pool receives the most tidal action. Organisms go through periods of no water followed by complete submergence in ocean water. Limpets, sea cucumbers, and sea palms often live in the middle portion. The lowest portion of a tide pool may only be exposed to air during very low tides. This part of the pool is the closest to a fully marine environment. Abalone, brown seaweed, and crabs often live in the lowest portion.

Tide pool in California

Thunderstorm over the Arizona desert

CHAPTER FOUR

AIR

The atmosphere is the layer of gases that surrounds the earth. Plants and animals use the gases to survive. The atmosphere acts like a giant filter, protecting life from harmful incoming radiation from the Sun. It also acts as a medium for weather to pass through. This chapter will explore what the atmosphere is made of and how weather and wind are created. Finally, it will explore the long-term effects of climate, especially on sensitive ecosystems.

Atmosphere

The atmosphere is mostly made up of nitrogen, oxygen, and argon (a colorless and odorless gas that does not react with other compounds).

The atmosphere around the young Earth had very little oxygen. Sunlight that reached the planet was not filtered, so the planet was showered with short-wavelength solar radiation. This radiation, like a bad sunburn, was destructive to life at the planet's surface. To survive, organisms lived deep in the mud or underwater for protection.

As the amount of oxygen increased in the atmosphere, the incoming short-wavelength solar radiation transformed oxygen to create a new molecule called ozone. Ozone is much better at absorbing short-wavelength radiation than oxygen. With the ozone in place, the surface of the earth became more habitable and organisms began to evolve and live in different regions on the planet's surface.

Earth's atmosphere consists of five distinct layers. The layers are defined by temperature and altitude, or their

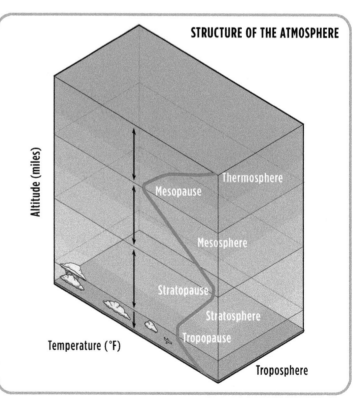

STRUCTURE OF THE ATMOSPHERE

Altitude (miles)

Temperature (°F)

Thermosphere

Mesopause

Mesosphere

Stratopause

Stratosphere

Tropopause

Troposphere

height above land. The troposphere is the layer closest to Earth's surface. It extends to roughly 7.5 miles above the surface of the planet. More than 75 percent of the planet's atmospheric mass is found in the troposphere, and it is the layer of the atmosphere where weather develops. Air temperature decreases through the troposphere with increasing altitude. The tropopause marks the top of the troposphere, where the air temperature reaches a minimum of around –94 degrees Fahrenheit.

The stratosphere extends from the tropopause to 31 miles above the surface of the planet. Most ozone is found in the stratosphere. Inside this layer, the temperature increases with higher altitude. The temperature difference between the stratosphere and the troposphere prevents the air from mixing between these two layers. At the top of the stratosphere, the temperature reaches a maximum of around 30 degrees Fahrenheit, marking the stratopause.

The next layer is the mesosphere. It extends from the top of the stratopause to about 50 miles above the planet's surface. Almost 99.9 percent of the mass of the atmosphere is contained below the mesosphere. The temperature decreases with increasing altitude. A minimum temperature of around –140 degrees Fahrenheit at the top of the mesosphere marks the mesopause.

The thermosphere extends from the top of the mesopause to 375 miles above the planet's surface. Incoming radiation from the Sun causes the temperature to increase dramatically with altitude. At the top of the thermosphere is the thermopause, where the temperature reaches 1,810 degrees Fahrenheit.

The exosphere is the outermost layer of the atmosphere. It extends from the top of the thermosphere to 120,000 miles above the surface of the earth. It is dominated by lighter gases, such as hydrogen, helium, carbon dioxide, and oxygen.

THE NITROGEN CYCLE

Nitrogen is a gas that you cannot see or smell and that is abundant in the atmosphere. It is also an essential element for making the building blocks necessary for life. Although nitrogen is abundant in the atmosphere, nitrogen in gas form is not easy for plants and animals to use. The nitrogen cycle describes the paths that different forms of nitrogen take as they move around the planet. Nitrogen gas transitions from forms that plants and animals cannot use to forms of organic nitrogen that they can use. Nitrogen is converted between different forms with the help of bacteria and lightning.

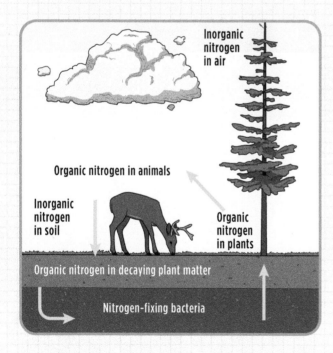

Wind

Gravity is a force that attracts an object toward another object's center of mass. Because Earth is so big, every object on and above the ground is attracted toward the planet's center. Gravity also affects air. Air pressure is the force exerted on an object, like the earth's surface, due to the gravitational pull of the air in the atmosphere. Atmospheric pressure decreases as the altitude increases. Air pressure can also change based on changes in temperature. Warm air has more energy for gas molecules to move farther apart, creating low pressure. Cold air has less energy, creating high pressure.

Global bands of air pressure are controlled by sunlight that enters the atmosphere. The equator has a band of low pressure. This region receives the most direct sunlight and the air is warm. The warm air rises into the atmosphere and flows both north and south. The air cools north and south of the equator at about one-third of the distance from the equator to the pole. The gas molecules in the cold air are closely spaced together, creating two parallel bands of high pressure that circle the globe. This air again flows north and south along the planet's surface. The air warms and eventually rises even further north and south of the equator. As the warm air rises, it forms a low-pressure band. The air again travels high in the atmosphere toward each pole. The cold air sinks again over each pole, producing a high-pressure system.

Air moves from an area of high pressure to an area of low pressure, like a ball rolling down a hill. As air moves, it produces wind. The speed of the wind depends on the difference in air pressure. A minor difference in air pressure produces a gentle breeze (12 miles per hour). An extreme difference in air pressure can result in a category-3 hurricane and violent winds (130 miles per hour).

The Coriolis effect is a force that causes a free-floating object to move to the right in the northern hemisphere (north of the equator) and to the left in the southern hemisphere (south of the equator). The bands of high and low pressure along Earth's surface produce global wind systems. In the northern hemisphere, the air flows toward the equator, but is deflected to the right. In the southern hemisphere, the air also flows toward the equator, but is deflected to the left. The resulting global wind system between is called the trade winds. The winds blow from northeast to southwest in the northern

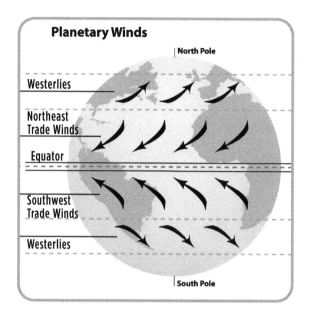

Planetary Winds

North Pole

Westerlies

Northeast Trade Winds

Equator

Southwest Trade Winds

Westerlies

South Pole

hemisphere and from southeast to northwest in the southern hemisphere. The westerlies generally blow from the west to the east. The polar easterlies generally blow from the east to the west.

Weather

Uneven heating of Earth's surface propels air to move through the atmosphere. Each air mass has a specific temperature, air pressure, and humidity conditions. Weather is generated when two or more air masses collide. Weather occurs along a front, which is the boundary between two air masses.

A cold front occurs when a cold air mass pushes into a warm air mass. The colder, denser air pushes the warmer, moister air higher into the atmosphere. Though air masses are invisible, the cold front is marked by cumulus or cumulonimbus clouds. Temperature often drops and the region experiences heavy rain.

A warm front occurs when a warm air mass pushes into a cold air mass. The warmer, moister air overrides the cold air mass. The front is marked by cirrus, cirrostratus, and altostratus clouds. Rain is common.

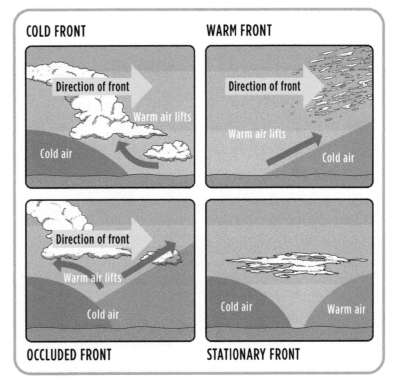

COLD FRONT

WARM FRONT

Direction of front

Warm air lifts

Cold air

Direction of front

Warm air lifts

Cold air

OCCLUDED FRONT

Direction of front

Warm air lifts

Cold air

STATIONARY FRONT

Cold air

Warm air

An occluded front occurs when a warm front becomes stuck between two cold fronts or vice versa. An occluded front brings precipitation to the region. Wind often changes direction as the different fronts pass through an area.

A stationary front forms when either a cold front or a warm front stops moving. This often happens when neither air mass is strong enough to push the other one out of the way.

A thunderstorm is a cloud characterized by lightning and fueled by moisture and unstable air. Warm, moist air rises into the atmosphere. Updrafts inject warm, moist air higher into the atmosphere. As the air cools, the water vapor condenses to liquid water droplets. The system continues to rise. As precipitation begins to fall from the cloud, cool

downdrafts form. Some storms will release microbursts, localized columns of sinking air. Wind speeds in microbursts can reach 100 miles per hour. A tornado is a narrow, spinning column of air that extends from the base of a cumulonimbus cloud to the ground. The largest storms have wind speeds exceeding 200 miles per hour.

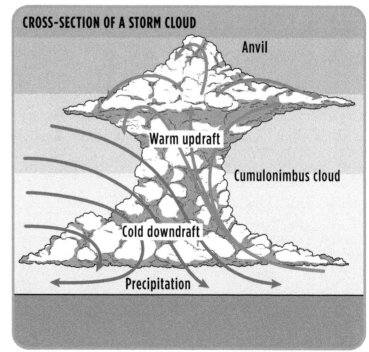

CROSS-SECTION OF A STORM CLOUD

Anvil

Warm updraft

Cumulonimbus cloud

Cold downdraft

Precipitation

Climate

Weather describes the physical, temperature, and humidity conditions in a region at a specific time. Climate is the 30-year average of weather conditions in an area. It is influenced by latitude, elevation, nearby bodies of water, ocean currents, topography, vegetation, and prevailing winds.

Solar radiation warms the planet unevenly because of Earth's tilted axis. The equator receives more consistent solar energy throughout the year than the poles. The uneven heating across the earth causes circulation patterns in the atmosphere. The movement of air in the atmosphere and water in the oceans transfers heat around the planet.

Global climate describes average long-term conditions over the entire planet. A period of warm conditions is described as a greenhouse climate. A period of cold conditions is described as an icehouse climate. The shift from warm to cold global climate conditions can take thousands to millions of years. The factors that often drive global changes in climate are important. Plate tectonics can take tens of millions or hundreds of millions of years to affect climate. Changes in Earth's position in its orbit around the Sun can take tens of thousands or hundreds of thousands of years to change climate. Changes in atmospheric chemistry can cause planetary warming in only a century. Greenhouse gases like water vapor, carbon dioxide, and methane trap heat near Earth's surface. In addition, these gases can linger in the atmosphere for tens to hundreds of years.

The result of changes in global climate can be devastating. In the historic record, changes in climate have been linked to crop failures, war, and mass migration. Recent human activities, like burning fossil fuels, have released abundant, ancient carbon

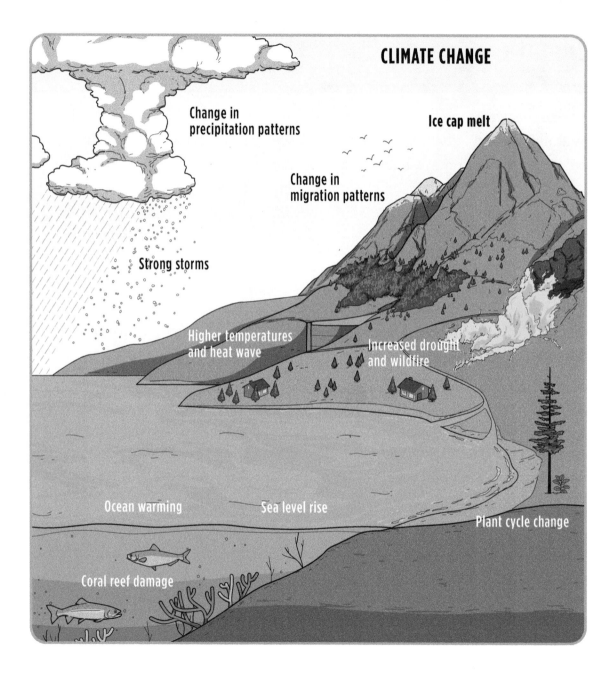

CLIMATE CHANGE

Change in precipitation patterns

Ice cap melt

Change in migration patterns

Strong storms

Higher temperatures and heat wave

Increased drought and wildfire

Ocean warming

Sea level rise

Plant cycle change

Coral reef damage

dioxide into the atmosphere. In the past century, global temperature has steadily increased. As a result, sea level is rising. Ice sheets are shrinking. Storms are becoming more powerful. Droughts and heat waves are common and precipitation patterns are changing.

HOW DO HURRICANES FORM?

Hurricanes are powerful storms. They begin as a low-pressure system over the tropical ocean. Warm ocean water adds energy to the overlying atmosphere by heat. As the energy increases, the pressure at the center of the storm decreases. Wind intensity increases as the pressure difference between the center of the storm and the outer perimeter of the storm increases. As wind intensity increases, the storm progresses from a tropical storm to a hurricane. A category-1 storm has maximum sustained wind speed from 119 to 153 miles per hour. A category-5 hurricane has sustained winds that are greater than 249 miles per hour. When the storm reaches land, it brings strong winds, storm surge, and heavy rainfall.

TORNADO IN A BOTTLE

A tornado is a powerful vortex that forms in the atmosphere. It is possible to recreate this phenomenon at home using a few household items. This activity will allow you to create and observe a vortex.

What You'll Need:

WATER

CLEAR PLASTIC BOTTLE WITH A CAP

LIQUID DISH SOAP

GLITTER

What to Do:

1. Pour water into a plastic bottle until it is three-quarters full.

2. Add 4 drops of liquid dish soap to the bottle.

3. Add a few pinches of glitter to the bottle.

4. Place the cap on tightly.

5. Turn the bottle upside down. Give it a quick spin in a circular motion. Gently place the bottle on a table. Watch a funnel form in the bottle!

ECOSYSTEM SPOTLIGHT

Climate change is having a profound effect on the planet. Mountainous regions are negatively affected by warming. An alpine biome is an important reservoir of freshwater. It is also home to many unique plant and animal species that have adapted to a cold environment with little rainfall. As the planet warms, plant and animal species are moving higher into the mountains to stay within their temperature range of comfort. Migrating higher into the mountains introduces new competitors to a smaller area for food and resources. Climate change also changes precipitation patterns so that less snow forms during the winter months. As the snowpack (layers of snow that add up over time) decreases, smaller amounts of snow melt each year, providing less drinking water to plants, animals, and communities at lower elevations.

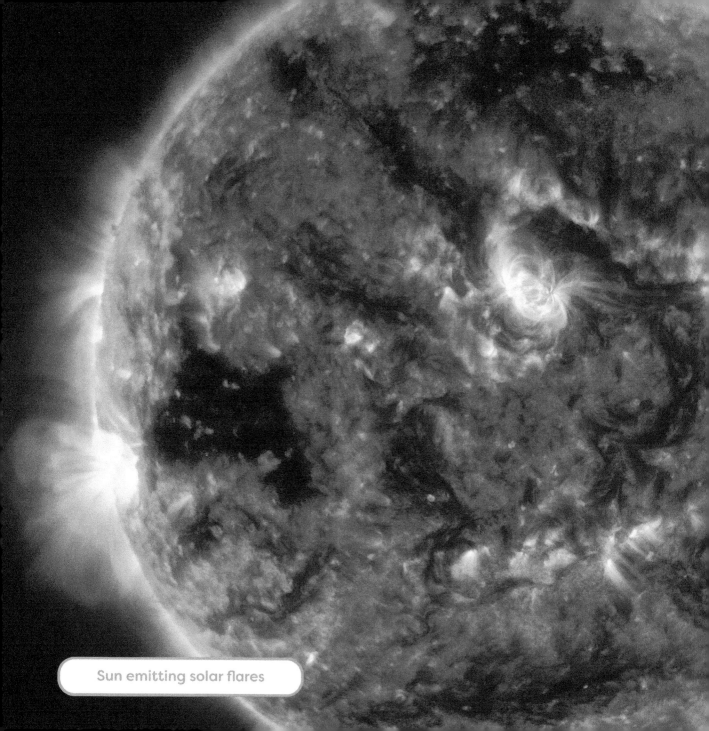

Sun emitting solar flares

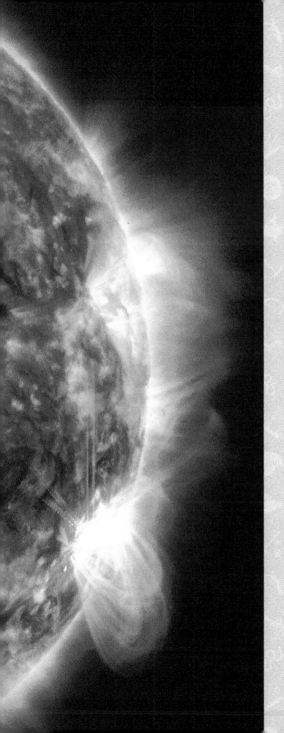

CHAPTER FIVE

SUN

The Sun is an ordinary star at the center of our solar system. It is similar to 100 billion other stars in our galaxy, the Milky Way. What makes the Sun special is its profound impact on Earth. It provides the energy that warms the surface of the planet. This energy also drives photosynthesis, which adds oxygen to the atmosphere and has made more complex and diverse life possible. The Sun drives weather. It also generates circulation in the atmosphere and ocean. This chapter will explore all of these themes to illustrate how important the Sun is to Earth.

What Is the Sun?

The Sun formed 4.5 billion years ago at the same time as the other planets in the solar system. It condensed from a cloud composed of the elements hydrogen and helium. This cloud was likely energized by an explosion from a nearby star. The cloud began to squeeze and shrink under the force of gravity. As this happened, pressure and temperature increased. Hydrogen and helium began to combine, causing them to ignite and form a star. This process led to the formation of gases found in very small amounts, like oxygen and nitrogen, and metals, such as iron and nickel.

The Sun is massive—333,000 times larger than Earth. Around 109 Earths could sit side-by-side across the width of the Sun. It's so big that it contains about 99.8 percent of all the mass in the entire solar system.

The Sun is composed of six layers. The core reaches temperatures in excess of 26,000,000 degrees Fahrenheit. The core is the factory where the Sun's fuel is made through a process called nuclear fusion.

The radiative zone encompasses about 50 percent of the Sun's radius. In this broad region, ions released from the core are absorbed and their energy is transferred via radiation to the outer convective zone. As this happens, the temperature cools at its outermost layer to 6,000,000 degrees Fahrenheit.

In the convective zone, heat is transferred by convection, which is the circulatory movement of heat in a fluid, like a gas or liquid. At the outer limits of the convective zone, the gases cool and sink where they are heated again.

The photosphere is the bright yellow surface that we know and recognize as the Sun. This region is thin, only 250 miles thick. It reaches temperatures close to 10,300 degrees Fahrenheit. Sunspots (dark patches on the Sun's surface), solar flares (big bursts of radiation), and solar prominences (plumes of spray ejected from the Sun's surface) form in the photosphere.

The chromosphere is the pinkish-red region of the Sun and is about 1,200 miles thick. The base of the chromosphere is actually the coolest part of the Sun, reaching just 6,300 degrees Fahrenheit. Moving higher into the chromosphere, the temperature increases to more than 60,000 degrees.

The corona is the outermost layer of the Sun. This wispy layer of gas can extend millions of miles into space. The gases are hot and fast. They burn close to 1,800,000 degrees Fahrenheit and move at around 550,000 miles per hour.

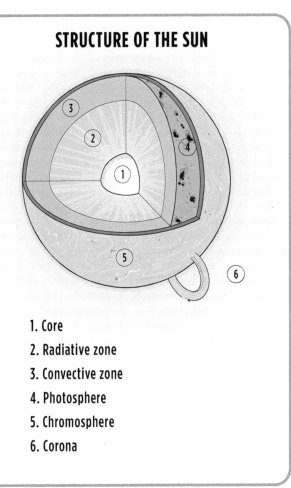

STRUCTURE OF THE SUN

1. Core
2. Radiative zone
3. Convective zone
4. Photosphere
5. Chromosphere
6. Corona

BUILD A SOLAR OVEN

You can make a pizza box into a solar oven. All you need are a few household materials and help from a grown-up.

What You'll Need:

LARGE PIZZA BOX

RULER

BLACK MARKER

BOX CUTTER OR UTILITY KNIFE

ALL-PURPOSE GLUE

ALUMINUM FOIL

SCISSORS

CLEAR PLASTIC WRAP

TAPE

BLACK CONSTRUCTION PAPER

POT HOLDER

TONGS

DRINKING STRAW

What to Do:

1. Draw a square on the pizza box lid, leaving a ¼-inch border around the edge.

2. Ask a grown-up to use the box cutter or utility knife to cut through three sides of the square.

3. Fold the newly cut-out flap back.

4. Glue the aluminum foil onto the underside of the flap.

5. Cut two square pieces of clear plastic wrap the same size as the lid.

6. Open the box lid and tape one piece of plastic wrap over the newly cut-out hole in the lid.

7. Close the box lid, lift the flap, and tape the second piece of plastic wrap over the hole in the lid.

8. Open the lid. Glue or tape a layer of aluminum foil to the inside of the pizza box.

9. Cover the foil inside the pizza box with black paper and glue it into place.

10. On a bright day, preheat the solar oven by placing it in direct sunlight for 30 minutes. It can reach 200°F. Make sure to have a grown up with you when the solar oven preheats.

11. Ask a grown-up to place a slice of leftover pizza in the solar oven, using a pot holder and tongs for safety. Adjust the solar flap to identify the best angle to capture the most sunlight. Use the straw to prop the flap open. Check on the food every 30 minutes, until it is hot. Have an adult help you take the pizza out of the solar oven.

Sunlight

Our planet's greatest energy source is the Sun. It takes 8 minutes and 20 seconds for sunlight to leave the Sun's surface and reach Earth. The planet does not absorb all incoming solar radiation. Some regions reflect sunlight back into space. The absorbed sunlight is radiated and conducted back into the atmosphere. Greenhouse gases in the atmosphere absorb the energy radiated from Earth's surface. The planet does not heat up or cool down because the sunlight that is absorbed is balanced by the sunlight that is reflected.

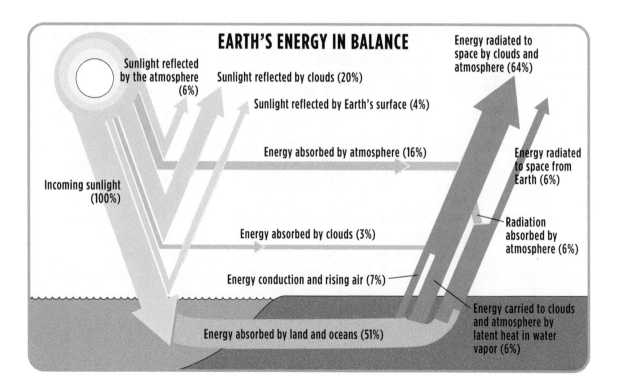

EARTH'S ENERGY IN BALANCE

Sunlight reflected by the atmosphere (6%)

Sunlight reflected by clouds (20%)

Sunlight reflected by Earth's surface (4%)

Energy radiated to space by clouds and atmosphere (64%)

Energy absorbed by atmosphere (16%)

Energy radiated to space from Earth (6%)

Incoming sunlight (100%)

Energy absorbed by clouds (3%)

Radiation absorbed by atmosphere (6%)

Energy conduction and rising air (7%)

Energy carried to clouds and atmosphere by latent heat in water vapor (6%)

Energy absorbed by land and oceans (51%)

PHOTOSYNTHESIS

Photosynthesis is the world's solar battery. Sunlight fuels organisms at the base of the food web. During this chemical reaction, plants, algae, and some bacteria convert carbon dioxide into food. Oxygen is produced as a byproduct of the chemical reaction. Solar energy is captured by plant matter, and this plant matter is eaten by herbivores (plant-eaters). This energy is also transferred to carnivores (animal-eaters) at higher levels of the food web.

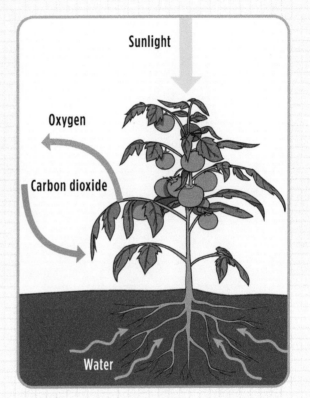

Sunlight

Oxygen

Carbon dioxide

Water

The Earth–Sun–Moon System

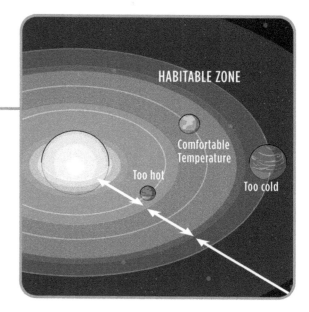

The Sun is the center of our solar system. It exerts a gravitational pull on all objects in the solar system. Consequently, everything in our solar system revolves around the Sun.

There are eight planets that revolve around the Sun, and Earth is the third planet from the Sun. Earth makes one trip around the Sun every 365.25 days. It rotates on its axis every 24 hours. The Moon revolves around Earth, completing one trip every 27 days. The Moon also rotates once on its axis in the same time that it takes to complete its trip around Earth. For this reason, people always see the same side of the Moon.

For a planet to have liquid water, it has to lie within the habitable zone of a solar system. If a planet is too close to the Sun, any liquid water would evaporate. If a planet is too far from the Sun, any liquid water would freeze. For example, the first planet in our solar system, Mercury, is too close to the Sun to be habitable. Water has boiled off the surface of the planet. Conversely, Mars, the fourth planet in the solar system, is too far from the Sun and water on its surface is frozen. Earth is in a perfect position in the solar system to have liquid water, which is essential for life.

WHAT IS A SOLAR ECLIPSE?

The Moon revolves around Earth. Earth revolves around the Sun. Occasionally, the three bodies align, producing a solar eclipse. During a solar eclipse, the Moon moves directly between Earth and the Sun. The Sun shines on the Moon and the Moon casts a shadow on Earth. The umbra is the shadow that blocks the entire view of the Sun. It only covers a small portion of the planet. Surrounding the umbra is a larger shadow, called the penumbra. Part of the Sun can be seen when viewed from within the penumbra. A person standing on land in the umbra experiences a total solar eclipse. During a total eclipse, the sky gets dark and transitions to twilight for 10 to 20 minutes during daylight hours. During this time, the temperature drops, and sometimes, stars become visible in the sky.

ECOSYSTEM SPOTLIGHT

Eight planets revolve around the Sun. The inner four planets—Mercury, Venus, Earth, and Mars—have solid, rocky surfaces. The outer four planets—Jupiter, Saturn, Uranus, and Neptune—are large, mostly gas- and ice-rich planets. Pluto was downgraded from planet status

in 2006. Today, it is classified as a dwarf planet. Our solar system is located within one of the spiral arms that make up the Milky Way galaxy. A galaxy is a collection of stars and their solar systems, all held together by gravity. The Milky Way is described as a barred spiral galaxy. The bar is the central core of the galaxy and the spiral arms, composed of stars and clouds of gas, revolve around the galactic center. Astronomers believe that our Sun is but one of billions of stars that exist within the galaxy. If there are billions of stars within the Milky Way galaxy, then there are billions of solar systems, and maybe some like ours, inside the galaxy.

MORE TO EXPLORE

BOTANICUM: WELCOME TO THE MUSEUM
BY KATHY WILLIS AND KATIE SCOTT

GEOGRAPHY: A VISUAL ENCYCLOPEDIA
BY DK CHILDREN

NATIONAL GEOGRAPHIC READERS: WATER
BY MELISSA STEWART

*NATURE JOURNAL: A KID'S NATURE
STUDY JOURNAL*
BY ALICE M. CANTRELL

*POCKET GENIUS: ROCKS AND MINERALS:
FACTS AT YOUR FINGERTIPS*
BY DK CHILDREN

GLOSSARY

ATMOSPHERE (AT-MUS-SFEER): the thin gaseous layer that surrounds Earth

BIOME (BI-OHM): a major ecological community type, such as tropical rain forest, grassland, or desert

BIOSPHERE (BI-O-SFEER): the global sum of all ecosystems, including all living organisms and their local environments on Earth

CLIMATE (KLI-MUT): the 30-year average course or condition of the weather for a specific location on Earth, which commonly considers temperature, humidity, atmospheric pressure, wind velocity, and precipitation

CRYOSPHERE (KRY-O-SFEER): all of the frozen components of the hydrosphere

EROSION (IH-ROH-ZHUN): the geological process through which sediment is transported across the earth's surface by natural forces, such as wind or water

GEOSPHERE (GEE-O-SFEER): any of the almost spherical concentric regions of matter that make up the earth and its atmosphere, such as the lithosphere and hydrosphere

GRAVITATIONAL FORCE (GRAV-I-TAY-SHUH-NUL FORS): the force of attraction between all masses in the universe; especially the attraction of the earth's mass for bodies near its surface

HYDROSPHERE (HI-DRO-SFEER): all water on, above, and below the earth's surface, whether in the form of liquid, gaseous vapor, or solid ice

IGNEOUS (IG-NEE-US): the type of rocks that form when magma or lava solidifies

INORGANIC (IN-OR-GAH-NIK): material that does not contain carbon

LAVA (LAH-VUH): molten rock that erupts from a fissure at Earth's surface

MAGMA (MAG-MUH): molten rock material within the earth from which igneous rock forms by cooling

METAMORPHIC (MEH-TUH-MOR-FIK): a type of rock formed when minerals in an older rock are changed by pressure and heat, becoming more compact and more crystalline

METAMORPHISM (MEH-TUH-MOR-FIZM): a change in a rock caused by changes in pressure and/or heat

MINERAL (MIN-UH-RULL): a solid crystal with a known composition that forms inorganically in nature

ORGANIC (OR-GAH-NIK): material that contains carbon

PHOSPHORUS (FOSS-FOR-US): a nonmetallic element of the nitrogen family with atomic number 15; occurs widely, especially as phosphates

SEDIMENTARY (SEH-DIH-MEN-TUH-REE): a type of rock formed by or from deposits of sediment

TECTONIC PLATE (TEK-TAH-NIK): fragments of a planet's lithosphere that can move across its surface

WEATHERING (WEH-THUR-ING): the physical disintegration and chemical decomposition of earth materials at or near the earth's surface

INDEX

ABOUT THE AUTHOR

Stacy W. Kish, MS, has always been

et's climate has changed over the past 160,000 years. For the past 15 years, she has worked as a science writer, preparing content for textbooks as well as academic and governmental websites. When Stacy is not writing, she whiles away the hours making cakes that inevitably are given to neighbors. She lives in Pittsburgh, Pennsylvania, with her street cat, the charismatic sidekick for the neighborhood.

CPSIA information can be obtained
at www.ICGtesting.com
Printed in the USA
JSHW011954021021
19124JS00001B/3